Michael Rodgers & Gi

Glendalough
A Celtic Soul Journey

St. Kevin's Church

Ciúnas Books

First published 2003, by

Ciúnas Books

Tearmann Centre
Brockagh,
Glendalough,
Co. Wicklow
Tel: 0404 - 45208
e-mail:micr@eircom.net

Cover Illustration by Padruig McFarlane-Barrow A.R.I.B.A
Illustrations by Padruig McFarlane-Barrow

Printed in Ireland by
Genprint Ireland Ltd, Clonshaugh, Dublin 17

ISBN 0-9544639-0-0

Annunciation

Eternal moments
When past and future become present
In this sacred place:
Voices of ages past speak,
Touching a depth of timelessness;

Echoes of monks chanting matins
In the early morning birdsong;
Noonday prayer
In the waters tumbling down the mountainside;
And the gentle whisper of the dying breeze
For vespers.

The ever-present mist speaks
Of Mystery
Which enfolds all things,
Lifts to allow tantalising glimpses
And falls again;

Waters spilling in glorious plenty speak
Of the extravagance of this Mystery
And every stone and plant and blade of grass
Becomes a burning bush;

No longer
"Listen Lord, Your servant is speaking" but
"Speak Lord,
        Your servant
                Is barefoot".

Pauline Corcoran.
Glendalough 25/3/98

Poulanass Waterfall in flood

Contents

Market Cross

Preface

At the beginning of the 21st Century in the midst of the communications revolution many people are experiencing feelings of disconnection and alienation. One response to this dilemma is a growing desire to rediscover roots and live in a more soulful way. In Ireland this search for soul is sometimes expressed in what has come to be known as Celtic spirituality.

My own search for my Celtic roots led me to Glendalough in 1992 after twenty years in Africa as a member of St. Patrick's Missionary Society. I was born and raised in a rural parish in East Clare called Killanena. I grew up in a family and among neighbours for whom Christianity was a way of life. Returning to Ireland in 1985 I saw my homeland with new eyes. I visited many of the ancient and early Christian monuments and recognised for the first time that my ancestors are an important part of who I am. It was a spiritual awakening that eventually drew me to live and work in the beautiful valley of Glendalough, where the monastery of St.Kevin was established in the sixth century.

The focus of my journey soon centred on the old An Oige hostel which had recently changed hands and was in the process of being converted into apartments by its new owners. The main part of the building has historical importance, as it was the first National School built in this part of the country in 1865. From the first renovated apartment, I began exploring the treasures and mysteries of the valley and writing down my reflections. These were included in a book called, *Glendalough a Celtic Pilgrimage*, which I co-wrote with Marcus Losack. It was edited by Gill McCarthy and published by Columba Press in 1996. A further development was that as the apartments became available at the converted An Oige hostel, I rented them from the owners to accommodate the increasing numbers of people who wished to stay for a while. Eventually my initiative occupied the whole complex and Tearmann [Sanctuary] Spirituality Centre was born.

One important development throughout the years has been a reflective pilgrimage walk around the monuments within the valley. Many people from twelve-year olds to retired older people take part in these walks. Secondary school students also visit for a one-day retreat experience. For these, Gill and I prepared a booklet with short reflections for the various points of interest and significance along the way. That was the first edition of this present book. Other people who read it liked the content and wanted a copy to take home so that they could keep alive the memories of their day's experience in Glendalough. As a result, in the year 1998, the fifteen hundredth anniversary of St. Kevin's birth, we decided to re-write the booklet, which we called *Glendalough, A Pilgrim Way.* This new book is a further development, which includes insights and understanding that we have gained from pilgrims we have met both in the house and on the road over the past ten years.

I would like to express my gratitude to Gill McCarthy, co-author and producer of this book, for her soul-friendship, inspiration and wisdom. We are indebted to Padruig McFarlane-Barrow for his beautiful illustrations, and for being such a sensitive, caring and creative spirit. A special word of thanks to Ray O'Sullivan, Denise McIntosh, Ken Brennan and the team at Genprint for their enthusiasm, helpful suggestions, skill and patience. I also acknowledge with great appreciation the poetic reflections given to me by people on retreat and by others attending a day's pilgrimage. We have taken extracts from some of their work and inserted them as little gems of insight adorning the main text.

We hope and pray that visitors to Glendalough will experience the chapters of this book as signposts guiding them on a spiritual journey through a special place. We offer the fruit of our work as a soulful, challenging and gentle companion to all who read it, wherever they are.

Michael Rodgers.

Glendalough

Tearmann Spirituality Centre

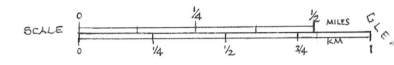

SCALE

CAMADERRY MOUNTAIN

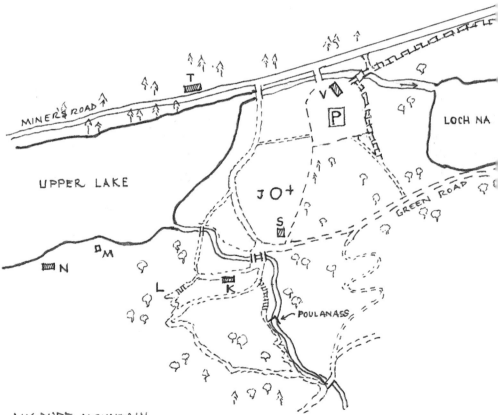

MINERS ROAD

UPPER LAKE

LOCH NA

GREEN ROAD

N

M

L

K

J O +

S

P

V

T

POULANASS

LUGDUFF MOUNTAIN

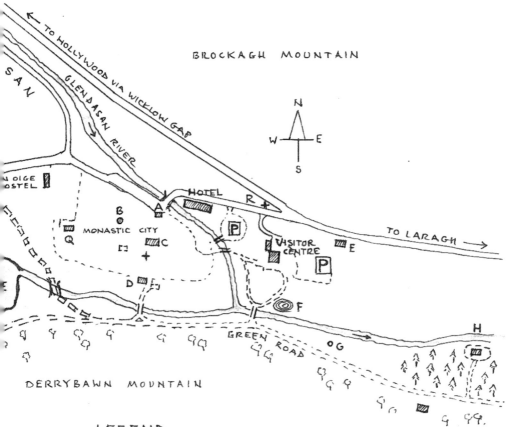

LEGEND

A	ENTRANCE GATEWAY	K	REEFERT CHURCH
B	ROUND TOWER	L	ST KEVIN'S CELL
C	CATHEDRAL	M	ST KEVIN'S BED
D	ST KEVIN'S CHURCH	N	TEAMPALL NA SKELLIG
E	TRINITY CHURCH	Q	ST MARY'S CHURCH
F	LABYRINTH	R	PILGRIM CROSS
G	ST KEVIN'S WELL	S	WILD LIFE INFO. CENTRE
H	ST SAVIOURS MONASTERY	T	EDUCATION CENTRE
J	CAHER	V	PUBLIC TOILETS
P	CAR PARK	□□□□□	BOARD WALK

Some Important Dates In The Story of Glendalough

Mid-6th Century: Kevin came to Glendalough and set up his hermitage on the shores of the upper lake.

618: Death of Kevin

789: Relics of Kevin removed to Monastic city, which had become the main centre of the community in Glendalough

837: Monastery plundered by Vikings

985: Monastery attacked by the Danes

1017 – 1163: Annals record repeated plundering and burning by foreigners and locals

1127: Birth of Laurence O'Toole

1153: Laurence O'Toole became abbot of Glendalough. Reforms began

1162: Laurence appointed first Irish Archbishop of Dublin

1214: King John grants Glendalough to Archbishop of Dublin. Grant rejected by O'Toole's and local clans of Wicklow. Glendalough attacked and laid waste by the Normans

1398: Forces of Richard II plundered the Abbey. The See of Glendalough continued to keep direct relations with Rome until the end of 15th Century. The last Bishop to be appointed by Rome was Dennis White, a Dominican friar who finally surrendered to the Crown and the Archbishop of Dublin in 1497

1535: Christopher St.Lawrence appointed Abbot of Glendalough by Henry VIII. He held the office until the suppression of the monasteries during the Reformation.

1810 - 1835: St. Kevin's Church used for worship by local Catholics

1865: New Catholic church built in Laragh, one mile distant from Glendalough.

1. Introduction

Gateway, Monastic City

Glendalough – A Unique Place

This sacred spot
Of sounds, songs and stories.
A refuge of souls,
A well of strength,
A sense of God.

[Liam Lacey]

Glendalough, a valley of two lakes is sometimes referred to as the jewel in the heart of the Wicklow Mountains. There is something enchanting about it that has attracted people for hundreds of years. Is it the beauty of the scenery and the wonderful walks within the valley and all over the mountains? Could it be a fascination with the old ruins of the monastery with all their memories and secrets? Perhaps it is just one of those special places where there is a sense that the dividing line between this world and the otherworld is almost transparent. It is without doubt a soulful place.

The early Christian monks who built the monastery were well aware that the environment of the valley breathed a positive energy. They were very conscious of natural forces when identifying locations for their settlements and built the monastery where the valleys and rivers meet. In fact, the site of the old monastery where the round tower now stands is a meeting place of three valleys. It is not surprising the place became a focal point for so many spiritual journeys and people felt at home within its peaceful surroundings.

The Attraction of the Past

Why are we so attracted to the past? Are we just trying to stop the clock and recapture some mythical memory? Or is it because we suspect that the wisdom of the past can offer us guidance for the future?

Celtic spirituality is being interpreted in many different ways nowadays and we have tried to address some of these themes, including an emphasis on the individual as well as the community, the importance of the natural world, the place of the feminine and the mystical sense of God's presence in life. There is a temptation to interpret history in a way that satisfies a passing fancy, so in this book we have tried to honour the historical facts where they have been available. For example, many people find Celtic spirituality attractive because it seems free of the constraints of institution. In fact, while the Celtic church differed from the rest of Europe at that time in organisation and ritual, it was a rigidly orthodox organisation firmly rooted in Scripture values. The Confessions of St. Patrick clearly show that his understanding of the grace of God was central to his theology. He saw himself as no more than an instrument, or witness, of the power of God in Christ, bringing salvation to people. There is no doubt that in the centuries after his death his followers were totally committed to the tradition he established.

What is 'Soul'?

Glendalough is an ideal place to focus on a soul journey. In this book we suggest that *soul* implies the sacred heart of life, which human beings have an orientation to consciously seek. Soul is a mysterious quality or way of being that involves value, belief, desire, inspiration, longing and spiritual hunger. In the human person it is expressed through awareness, sensitivity, creativity and wonder. We believe that soul manifests itself most readily in the here-and-now experience of every day.

Your Journey begins

You are invited to enter the valley itself as a pilgrim and soul-seeker. We have posed questions throughout the text as a guide and invitation. Hopefully questions of your own will arise and we encourage you to stay with them. As you start your journey you may wish to ponder these questions:

'Where have I come from?'

'What am I looking for?'

'Why do we suffer?'

'What is my deepest longing?'

This enclosed valley will draw you into a deep, quiet place within yourself. During your visit be conscious of the harmony all around you and the many expressions of God's gratuity. Pray with reverence for everything you will experience as you discover the treasures of this holy ground. Take time to stand and stare. Your presence here is important, adding another link to the ongoing revelation of the story of this special place.

2. Pilgrimage

I journey outward
Leaving home;
A step forward
Into newness;
A step
Into the unknown

[Liam Lacey]

The Tradition of Pilgrimage

Throughout history, and woven into the traditions of many religions, pilgrimage has always attracted large numbers of people, both as a personal search and quest, but also as an experience to be shared with others. From the time of Christ, Jerusalem has attracted pilgrims, likewise Mecca which has the most famous pilgrimage of all known as the Hadji. Ireland has many pilgrimage centres including Croagh Patrick and Lough Derg, which were identified as holy places in pre-Christian times. Glendalough became an important place of pilgrimage when the Celtic monastery of St. Kevin flourished from the 6th to the 12th centuries. Long after the monasteries closed, and especially in the 17th and 18th centuries when there were very few churches or places of worship, visiting the ancient sacred sites became an important expression of people's spirituality. Over the years, Glendalough became a principal centre of pilgrimage in the province of Leinster.

The journey to the sacred place was just as important as the arrival. Pilgrims endured much discomfort on the way over rough land and water in order to reach their destination. Some left home never to return. This was known as the white martyrdom. Others remained around holy places dedicating their lives to God as monks and nuns. Pilgrimage at this level was undertaken for the high motive of the love of God or the salvation of souls.

There is an old story that tells of a boat carrying Irish monks being washed ashore on the coast of Cornwall. When asked where they were going, they replied that they had stolen away because they wanted to be on pilgrimage for the love of God. For those early monks and missionaries, pilgrimage was a penitential journey living out the difficult choice of the call to follow Christ.

A Personal Quest

Most people who went on pilgrimage however, had a more practical purpose in mind. They were happy to visit a holy place once a year or once in a lifetime. They went with a specific intention in mind. It was usually to ask a favour or come to terms with some mishap or misfortune they had suffered. They would share their stories as they travelled along the road, and the listening ear accompanying them would be an important part of the experience. We all have a desire to be heard and understood and need support and encouragement. Nobody would be ignored or excluded, and those who were vulnerable, including the young, the old and the sick would be given special attention and help. The pilgrim's wish for healing, better fortune, forgiveness and freedom from negative and soul-destroying preoccupations would eventually be placed at the pilgrimage shrine in the form of prayers and offerings. At the heart of the experience lay a longing and conviction that by travelling to a special place they might somehow be strengthened and renewed.

The Spirituality of Pilgrimage Continues

The spirituality of pilgrimage is again striking a chord in the modern world. We are moving from a period when religious expression became somewhat controlled to a time when we want to explore our own spirituality in different ways. Pilgrimage has an open and unpredictable aspect that is attractive, possibly reflecting the reality of most people's lives. It sets out with a definite purpose or end in view but once the journey begins the open road determines what happens next. It is possible to take a wrong turn or lose the way and unexpected hazards and obstacles will appear from time to time. The pilgrim journey is never static but ever-changing and always new.

The very heart of pilgrimage is about the restlessness of the human spirit, which is always seeking and yet paradoxically longs to be at home. The outer journey over the landscape often reflects the inner landscape of the soul's journey. They are not two different events, but a single one with two perspectives, and images from the natural world can help activate our spiritual imagination. For example, Glendalough has a dark side that rarely sees the sun and also an open, brighter aspect. It is a place to enjoy the beauty and blessing of creation but also to be aware of the pain of carrying the cross.

As a pilgrim you are invited on an adventure into your inner being and we encourage you to accept all you find there. This is difficult for most of us. It is however, the way we are most likely to find the freedom to live in a creative, connected and appreciative way. In this booklet we use the word 'journey' to describe meaning or purpose as well as distance travelled and years lived. *What point have you reached on your journey? What anxieties and tensions are you carrying with you? Are you open to all that awaits you?*

A Dhia, beannaigh an chéim
a bhfuil mé ag dul.
Beannaigh dom an chré
atá fém ' chois.

O God, bless the step
that I am taking,
and bless the soft earth
beneath my feet.

[Old Irish Prayer]

3. The Story of Kebin

St. Kevin at Prayer

Historical facts about the life of St. Kevin are few and far between. The only date regarded as reliable is the date of his death which is given in the Annals of Ulster as 618 A.D. It is important to remember that the stories about Kevin's life were handed on firstly by oral tradition, only to be written down much later. There were five Lives of St. Kevin written in Irish and Latin hundreds of years after his death. The earliest of these in Latin dates from the 11th. Century and is completely lacking in historical content. People who wrote the lives of the saints long after they lived tended to exaggerate and invent stories to support their own outlook and purpose. As a result more legend than fact was written. However, stories, myths and legends survive primarily because they express deeper truths that the heart understands, and so provide valuable insights into all our lives.

We can be fairly certain that Kevin existed and that he lived in Glendalough. The legends tell us that he was born into a noble family and an angel visited his mother during her pregnancy indicating she would give birth to a boy who would be close to God and a great leader. He was extraordinarily gifted and at the age of twelve his parents sent him for training to three holy mentors, Eogan, Lochan and Enna at the monastery of Kilnamanagh, which was probably located near Tallaght in County Dublin.

A Restless Dreamer

It seems there was a restless spirit in Kevin from an early age and a desire to follow his dreams. One story recounts how he ran away from the monastery and hid in the Wicklow Mountains, eventually finding his way to Glendalough where he lived an austere and simple life in the hollow of a tree, completely dependant on the natural world around him for sustenance. After a time he was discovered in his hiding place and brought back to the monastery where he was ordained a priest by Bishop Lugid. Some time later he set out again with a few companions to found a new monastery at Cluainduach. From there he returned to Glendalough and set up his hermitage.

What was the dream and spirit inside Kevin that drew him to Glendalough? Why would a young man from a privileged home be prepared to leave all the supports and benefits of that background? Perhaps he felt the need to strip himself of the trappings of his life in order to find his own soul. He was apparently attracted to the mystical experience of eremitic life. The discovery of the old Bronze Age tomb on the side of the cliff above the upper lake offered this longing a focus and place.

Stories and Legends

Perhaps the best we can do in this short account of the life of Kevin is to look at a few of the legends and stories about him and explore something of the meaning behind them. Some of these narratives are timeless. They can be found in various forms in religious traditions throughout the world. The spiritual questions of people everywhere are very similar.

Kevin is always described as having a close affinity with the natural world. The best-known story is about Kevin and the blackbird, which we will recount later. A frightened, hunted boar once took refuge in his cell while the dogs pursuing it lay down outside. On another occasion he was praying while standing in the cold waters of the lake and dropped his book in the water. It was quickly recovered and returned to him by an otter. He is described in contemplation beneath a tree with many birds perched upon his head and shoulders. All of these stories suggest in a tender way that the human person at prayer joins earth with heaven. In all these stories, Kevin comes across as a prayerful and spiritual man, full of love, gentleness, respect and care for the earth and its creatures.

St. Kevin and Blackbird
Sculpture: Imogen Stuart

We have already referred to Kevin's restlessness that continued throughout his life. Once, when he was well advanced in years and planning a pilgrimage, a holy man called Garban challenged him with the words "It is better for you to remain in one spot, serving the Lord, than to go about from place to place in your old age: for you have heard that no bird, while flying, can hatch her eggs" [John O'Hanlon, *Lives of the Irish Saints*, Vol.6, James Duffy & Sons, Dublin,1891]. Towards the end of his life it is related that an angel came to persuade him to move to a new location. After much discourse he agreed, but when they arrived at the appointed site he questioned its suitability because it was strewn with large stones. A lot of people today would identify with Kevin's restlessness and questioning but also his stubborn belief in his own opinion. Perhaps he was one of the original rugged and rare individuals who are courageous enough to stand out from the crowd and as a result bring about significant changes in all our lives.

The legends about Kevin's life often recount his experience of solitude in his desert. There are tales of devils tempting him to give up his quest and angels coming to support and comfort him. In spite of everything he persevered in his eremitic life. Paradoxically, the events of his life also show he was a charismatic and effective leader, sharing his gifts in the founding of religious communities. In a time when leaders are often perceived as prestige hungry and personally ambitious, it is intriguing to hear of a person who took on a leadership role regularly, but was also able to walk away from it.

Kevin and Kathleen

It is apparent that Kevin was a man who struggled throughout his life with conflicting longings. One area would have been his choice to live celibately. There is a well-known story that dramatically illustrates this personal struggle. A young girl was very attracted to him and made passionate advances. He rushed away from her and rolled naked in a bed of nettles having stripped off all his clothes. When the girl arrived and witnessed this extraordinary behaviour, he beat her away with the stinging nettles until she fell on her knees begging for forgiveness. Afterwards, she decided to dedicate herself entirely to God by entering religious life. This is a tale about two young people ardently attracted to each other while at the same time feeling that they had to choose between that desire and a wish to give their lives to God.

This episode illustrates the real struggle in Kevin's quest for holiness. It is a poignant tale of rejecting human love for something perceived as greater. It is possible to appreciate the depth and beauty of the incident, with all its passion and longing, and at the same time understand his response as a gesture born of great pain and deep appreciation for all that he was relinquishing. Kevin's inclination would be to live life to the full. Accounts of his life are evidence of that. His action of running naked into the nettles and then beating the girl with them could be seen to be the action of someone full of longing, desire and ambivalence. How often are we overcome with longing for what cannot be ours if we are to remain true to our deeper selves? We are all ambivalent in many different ways.

Nearly every person who comes to Glendalough has heard this story and wants to know more about it. The original version of events is not told any more and what has emerged in its place is a tale that concludes with a woman called Kathleen drowning in the lake, having been thrown in by Kevin from the cliff at St. Kevin's Bed. Kathleen is a modern name, which appeared first a hundred years ago in a poem written by Thomas Moore. The fact that this is the key account that interests visitors, even though they find it abusive and laughable, suggests that perhaps we are often amused by our own contradictions.

The Legend of Kevin Lives on

What is the enduring attraction that continues to fascinate us about Kevin all these centuries later? Is it because the stories of his life are archetypal? We all struggle with conflicts and contradictions that pull us in different directions. Most of us are caught at some time between our commitments to others and our longing to follow our dreams. We desire solitude yet need the company and affirmation of relationships. We yearn for harmony, but too often find ourselves discordant and abrasive. Above all, we seek meaning in our lives and want to be true to ourselves. Kevin intrigues us because of the extremes he endured to find and live a life of meaning and personal truth.

There is much of Kevin's story that is yet to be explored. We have only shared a little of it here. As we walk in his footsteps, may we find encouragement and inspiration. His struggles can illuminate our struggles and the peace he found become our peace. Let his dream give us hope and the courage to follow our own dreams.

Ever-living, Loving God,
Long ago you led the young man
Kevin, to the beautiful valley of
Glendalough to follow his dream,
And grow in knowledge of himself
and union with you through
presence, prayer and penance.

Help us treasure life as he did,
accepting all its shades of light and
darkness. In our busy world may we
find a little space to be still
and know you are our God.

4. Trinity Church

Hallowed stones, signs of a people
Present long ago,
Their dreams founded on things sacred.
I, another pilgrim with another dream
Touch the stones,
I stand encircled by them.

[A pilgrim to Glendalough]

Trinity Church

21

A Thousand Year Old Treasure

The first stop on this pilgrim soul journey is the 11th century church of the Trinity. It is one of the finest examples we have in Ireland of an old stone church. Climbing over the stile from the road and descending the steps to the church is quite difficult for some people and they may need others to give them a hand. *Do you find it hard to ask for assistance?*

The stone steps leading down to the church are a reminder of ancient origins. The dark stone called mica schist was laid down under the sea some 500 million years ago. The bottom step of lighter shade is granite, which came from the core of the earth in a molten state 380 million years ago. It cooled slowly and therefore is a very dense, hard rock. This stone is found in the doorway, the archway and the cornerstones of the church. It forms the heart of the Wicklow Mountains which overlook Glendalough.

Only local stones were used to build the church of the Trinity. Each stone was cut and shaped and put in place by skilful, devoted hands all those years ago. Touch the stones and be attentive to the echoes of memory within them. If these stones could speak what a story they would tell! Perhaps they only need someone to listen carefully for them to reveal their secrets.

When we consider ourselves within the great time span marked by the stones, we realize how short our lives are but also how privileged and challenged we are as human beings called to be guests and guardians of the earth. Psalm 8 recounts movingly how God appointed human beings rulers of all creation, suggesting that we have been given the responsibility not to exploit the natural world and each other but to protect and nurture all of life. Take a moment to ponder the question *'What is my response to this great and beautiful world in which I live?'*

Here and there between the stones of the old church walls a variety of lichens, ferns and occasional wild flowers grow. Looking back toward the steps you descended, you will notice the remains of another set of steps by the gnarled roots of an old ash tree. That tree was cut at some stage but new growth has sprung from its roots. All of life has such an instinct to survive and flourish. Become aware of how all the steps of your life have been nourished and influenced and changed along the way.

Doing the Rounds

There is a custom in Ireland of doing rounds at sacred sites. The Christian direction is 'deiseal' [clockwise] which moves to the right following the journey of the sun from east to west. This circular round gathers the energy of the four directions and connects all the steps of the journey. In ancient times the sun was understood to be the source of life and this belief continued for early Christians who looked to the sun as a symbol of the Risen Christ. Walk seven times around the church, noticing how the view changes at every corner, and be aware how even a slight change of perspective can make all the difference. Allow every movement that you make be a prayer.

Reflecting on an Ancient Symbol

Inside the church, go first into the annexe at the western end and stand facing the original doorway, which has remained intact for ten centuries. Notice there are three large granite stones on the right hand side and four on the left of different shapes and sizes. In religious tradition seven is the complete number. It is quite obvious there was a purpose and symbolism in the way these stones are placed which we may never fully understand. Symbols are open to interpretation however, and meaning can be found in them not even intended by the designer. Perhaps the doorway is a symbol of life itself with each stone representing a ten-year time span? Could the four stones on the left represent the first forty years of life when the emphasis is on achievement and exploring life's possibilities in every direction? The three stones in the right hand side of the doorway are clearly centred on the large one in the middle. Is this drawing attention to the second half of life when the call is to be more focused in oneself? Touch the stones in the doorway in turn while reflecting on the events and decades that have made up your life.

Passing through the doorway into the church, notice how the little window in the sanctuary space opens in the direction of the rising sun. This space in old churches always faced east and when priest and people worshipped God they faced east together. The archway spanning the area between the nave and the sanctuary is made up of fifteen well-shaped granite stones – seven on either side of the keystone. The stones on either side could represent the opposite experiences of life – light and darkness, joy and sorrow, success and failure. It is often mentioned that the strength of the old spirituality was the ability of people to hold in balance the varied experiences of their lives. Count the many blessings and disappointments of your life and ask yourself if you are holding them in a balanced way. A simple ritual to embody this reflection is to stand or kneel under the archway, and lift each outstretched arm slowly until the two hands join under the keystone, where the balance is held. Stay still in that position for a while. Perhaps you might like to design your own ritual.

Christ and the Trinity

We need to hold a balance personally but also communally. Irish spirituality was always firmly rooted in family. The doctrine of Three Persons in One God was acceptable to the Celts because it symbolised God as Trinity and community. Pre-Christian Celts regarded the number three as having special significance. Part of this religious tradition was belief in a triple goddess.

An old Irish prayer expresses the Christian understanding of the Triune God very well:

Praise to the eternal Father who created us
Praise to the only Son who ransomed us
Praise to the Spirit who blesses us
Praise to you, Trinity, one God only

The sense of God and Christ's presence pervading everything may be said to be the core belief of Celtic Christianity. It is expressed powerfully in the Breastplate Prayer of St. Patrick. For many Christians the day began with this prayer, invoking the mighty strength of the Trinity, in all its aspects, to protect them through the day from the forces of evil that were very real to them. Why not spend some time in Trinity Church praying and reflecting on this ancient prayer? *What protection would you like to ask for?*

> *Be Christ this day my strong protector;*
> *Against poison and burning,*
> *Against drowning and wounding,*
> *Through reward wide and plenty...*
> *Christ beside me, Christ before me;*
> *Christ behind me, Christ within me;*
> *Christ beneath me, Christ above me;*
> *Christ in my lying, my sitting, my rising;*
> *Christ in the heart of all who know me,*
> *Christ on the tongue of all who meet me,*
> *Christ in the eye of all who see me;*
> *Christ in the ear of all who hear me.*

[From The Deer's Cry: translation Noel D. O'Donaghue
- *An Introduction to Celtic Christianity,* editor James P. Mackey.
Publisher T & T Clarke, Edinburgh 1989].

Psalm 131
Eph 1: 3-10

5. The Green Road
– A Nature Walk

Blue-grey morning mists
seep through mountain pines
drifting as smoke
from dreamfires.

[Bernadette Knopek]

The Green Road

Life as a Labyrinth

Close to Trinity church is the Glendalough Visitor's Centre. It is well worth a visit to view the exhibits and the audio-visual, 'Ireland of the Monasteries'. As you leave the centre and walk toward the river, near to the bridge you will find a labyrinth set in the grass.

Labyrinths have been around for over 4000 years and are found in just about every major religious tradition in the world. Twelve miles from Glendalough near Hollywood on the western side of the Wicklow Mountains the oldest labyrinth stone in Ireland was discovered. It was placed at a point on the pilgrim road where a dangerous and difficult part of the journey over the mountains began. Perhaps it was placed there to warn pilgrims to be careful, but also as an encouragement that if they persevered the road would eventually lead them to their destination.

From the time of Christ, Jerusalem was a centre of Christian pilgrimage. During the Crusades in the 12th Century however, it became the focus of religious struggle and travel there became dangerous and expensive. At that time some European cathedrals were appointed pilgrimage centres.

Labyrinths were created in those cathedrals [e.g. Chartres in France] and the path of the labyrinth was known as the 'road to Jerusalem'. The walking of these cathedral labyrinths marked the ritual ending of the journey to the holy place.

We recommend spending time in the labyrinth. You might like to pray or meditate as you walk its path. The entrance leads in to the third circle and from there it flows gently outwards and inwards on a single path until it reaches the centre. Unlike a maze, the labyrinth has no dead ends. It has a beginning and end with many unexpected turns along the way. All the different movements and directions taken within it are a reminder that life itself is like a labyrinth. Be aware of how you approach the experience. *Does your response reflect the way you meet opportunities in your life?*

A Walk in Nature

Across the bridge over the river the way leads on to the Green Road. For the purpose of this soul journey we have decided to turn left and walk first to the twelfth century monastery of St. Saviour which was the last of the Glendalough churches to be built. Our intention is to begin a journey there, and then go back through space and time to the sixth century hermit's cell of St. Kevin near the shores of the upper lake.

The beginning of this journey is a walk through a beautiful natural environment. Celtic Christians liked to glorify God through His creation. People cherished, respected and appreciated the created world because they believed that all things were in God. Their lives, prayers and rituals were intrinsically bound up with the rhythms of the seasons and the cycles of life. Everyday events such as lighting the fire, making the bread, planting the crops, eating food, putting the children to bed at night or going on a journey were all performed with an accompanying prayer and invocation of God's blessing.

On the road to St. Saviour's we are facing east, the

direction of the rising sun, which is the source of life's energy. In spring, the natural world here is alive with fresh new growth and colour bursting from the bleak emptiness of winter. As the heat of the sun increases, the earth comes alive with the brilliant yellow flowers of gorse turning the hedgerows into gold. Spring's spiritual gift is new beginnings and a promise of rebirth. There is a kind of secret revelation going on during this season which is spontaneous and full of promise. *What new promise would help you find rebirth?*

The best time to walk along the Green Road is in the early morning to catch some of the miracles of a new day. Then grasses are often bent heavy with dew, and spiderwebs create sparkling patterns laced through the vegetation. These webs look so delicate but in fact are extremely strong and can withstand winds and rain. Their intricate designs, which differ with each 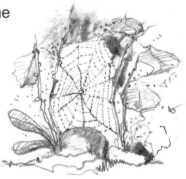 species of spider, are a reminder of the threads and complexities that connect us in our world of friendships and relationships, and of how enduring the most delicate thread can actually be.

The hills all around are hundreds of millions of years old, even though they didn't take on their present shape until they emerged from under the glaciers that covered both hills and valleys up to twelve thousand years ago. When those same glaciers melted they deposited huge boulders of granite here and there on the surface of the ground. Many of these can be seen near the sides of the Green Road.

There are trees everywhere and the clear running water of the river is never far away. One of the most rare and beautiful sights to come across is a mountain deer drinking water from the river. Many animals make their homes in these woods including the reclusive badger, the ever-vigilant fox and both red and grey squirrels, which stop people in their tracks when they appear. It is fascinating to observe them scampering easily up the trunks of trees and along the thinnest of branches. The great abundance and diversity of life in Glendalough creates a remarkable atmosphere of harmony and peace. It is impossible not to become aware that there is a bigger picture where we are one life form amongst many others.

The Beauty of Birds

Bashful jay
Your brazen cousins
Magpie, jackdaw and crow
Forever strut and show
Their arrogance and insolence.
You keep to yourself
Hiding your beauty
And cry aloud.

[Michael Rodgers]

Jay

As your awareness heightens, you may notice other creatures make their home here too. If you are lucky you will see rare birds like the jay, the treecreeper and the tiny goldcrest which is almost invisible among the trees and grasses. The amazing dipper goes underwater to find its food in the river, whilst the motionless heron waits patiently in shallow pools. In May, the call of the cuckoo echoing through the valley lifts the hearts of visitors who haven't heard its voice for years.

Some of the birds to be seen are yearlong residents, but others come and go according to the season. The phenomenon of migrating birds is extraordinary and fascinating. What causes them to suddenly take to the skies, flying the same routes as their ancestors? Do they use landmarks and even stars to guide them to their destination?

The Gift of Trees

Let me not spoil one leaf, nor break one branch
Let me not plunder, blunder, pollute, exploit
But rather see and hear and touch and taste and smell
And in my sensing, know you well, Creator God.

[Marie Connolly]

All this area forms part of the Wicklow Mountains National Park and offers an opportunity to enjoy one of Ireland's finest semi-natural woodlands. Above the road many oak trees grow individually and in groves. The oak is our national tree which covered most of the country until it was finally cut away in the seventeenth century. Many Irish place names have the word Derry in them coming from the Gaelic name for the oak tree which is 'crann daireach'. In ancient Ireland, it was believed that the spirits of the ancestors lived in the oak trees and prayers were offered and rituals performed within the oak groves. Within the environment they create today prayer still comes easily.

Trees make a symbolic link between earth and sky. Their roots can connect us with our earthy experience while the branches can represent our longing to reach out into the light. Just as every tree grows a little differently depending on the amount of light and space it receives, so our uniqueness is shaped by the circumstances of our lives. Trees grown for commercial purposes are planted close together. They grow straight and tall, which is helpful in their felling and processing. However, in forcing them to uniformity they have a limited life span compared to trees allowed to develop with more space. Could that be true for us too?

Stand with an individual tree that has been given a space to grow or stand deep within the forest of trees. Be aware that trees lived on this earth long before humans. We need them more than they need us. They provide us with shelter, food and fuel, and they purify the air we breathe. Look around at all you see. Close your eyes. Try to experience this place through your other senses. What can you hear, smell, touch and taste? Be still for a time. Open your eyes again. Do you experience any difference in the way you are seeing? *Ask yourself, what can I do to take care of the earth?*

For my shield this day I call:
Heaven's might,
Sun's brightness,
Moon's whiteness,
Fire's glory,
Lightning's swiftness,
Wind's wildness,
Ocean's depth,
Earth's solidity,
Rock's immobility.

[From The Deer's Cry: translation
Noel D. O'Donaghue]

Psalm 42 & 104
Gen 1 & 2

6. The Monastery of St. Saviour

Intimations of light,
an aperture, God's window.
The Abbey, solitary and serene,
nestled on a carpet of green,
circled by succulent trees.

[Catherine Campbell]

St. Saviour's Church

St. Saviour's church is signposted on the left hand side of the Green Road one kilometre away from the old monastery of Glendalough. From the road a pathway descends through rows of conifer trees. It can be disconcerting at first to enter the shadowy interior of the wood and there are roots of trees to stumble over unless care is taken. However, one quickly becomes aware of light in a clearing not far away which is the site of St. Saviour's. A circle of tall trees surrounds the ruins of the old church and monastery.

It is a good idea to go around to the back of the monastic site where there is easier access compared to the rather steep stile that you find in front when your arrive. Once you get to the top of the wall, slowly make the traditional circular walk all around the earthen bank which surrounds the building. By doing this you will get an overall view. Take time to ask the question, *what is the story of this place?*

12th Century: The End of an Era and a New Beginning

The story actually began in the twelfth century, which was a time of great change in Ireland. The Normans arrived on these shores in 1169 and with them a continental European influence that had been absent from Ireland during the preceding centuries. They introduced a new political system, which led to changes in social and religious institutions as well. This marked the beginning of the decline of the old Irish culture and language.

From the middle of the fifth century Ireland was divided into a few large dynasties ruled by families of the northern and southern Uí Neill at Grianán Aileach in Donegal and Tara in Meath. The southern part of the country was under the control of another dynasty, which had its residence in Cashel. Each of these kingdoms was divided into a number of smaller kingdoms based on the 'tuath' or tribe. All of these owed their allegiance to the higher kings and paid tribute to them. People's lives were family-based in a rural environment within a hierarchical society.

The old Irish monastic church which flourished for six hundred years was rooted in the social and political system of that time. The basic centre of organisation was not the diocese but the monastery which was modelled on the self-contained homesteads of the landowners. There were hundreds of monasteries scattered throughout the country, many of them quite small. This system was in decline by the middle of the twelfth century when Lawrence O'Toole became abbot of Glendalough in 1153. He saw the need for reform and change and invited the Canons of St. Augustine from France to establish a new monastic order which had already been tried and tested on the European mainland. They made clear their intention to establish something new by moving a considerable distance away from the old monastery. The new monastery later became known as St. Saviours.

Laurence O'Toole – Reformer

Laurence O'Toole was the son of a local ruler from Castledermot in Kildare who owed allegiance to the king of Leinster, Dermot MacMurrough, who lived in Ferns, Co Wexford. As a young boy he was fostered to that king

Doorway at St. Saviour's

which in reality meant that he was held as a hostage and treated harshly to ensure his father's submission and loyalty. He was eventually reunited with his father through the mediation of members of the monastery of Glendalough where he had stayed for some time. He felt so attracted to life in the monastery however, that he decided to join the community as a monk rather than return home. Laurence obviously had outstanding qualities because he was appointed abbot at the age of twenty-five. During his nine-year term of office he distinguished himself as a man of prayer who was deeply concerned for the poor. He also became renowned for his diplomatic skills after he became the first Irish Archbishop of Dublin in 1162 at a time of political and social upheaval throughout Ireland.

Changing Times

Inside the monastery, take time to sit and listen to the echoes of its story. Consider the difference between the simplicity of the old Celtic arch in Trinity church and the more elaborate richly decorated Hiberno-Romanesque arch that is here. The people who built this monastery were open to change and the value of outside influences but in the process they also lost some of the spontaneity and inclusivity of the past by trying to distance themselves from it. The three pillars supporting the right-hand side of the archway are the most authentic part of this old building. They illustrate some of the changes that were taking place. Part of the decoration is clearly Celtic, while more of it is expressing the European heritage. Change must include the best that the past has to offer while introducing what is an appropriate expression for the present. *How do you respond to change?*

It is possible to feel safe and comfortable within the precincts of St. Saviour's monastery. Life here was more controlled and centralized than the old monastic system that it replaced. It is likely that the whole community lived within the one complex of buildings. *What model of leadership do you prefer?*

Our time is a time of many changes but perhaps no more than the changes that took place in the twelfth century. Look at the ancient stones in the walls and the loose stones gathered at the western end of the church. Do we want to build on the past, or start again completely anew? *What kind of new expression would you like to see and who would you like to see included within it?*

You could stay for a long time in this quiet secluded place pondering these and many other questions. Perhaps a journey back through time and space to the old monastery of Glendalough, and then even further back to the sixth century hermitage of St. Kevin will help us find some answers.

Ever living, Loving God,
May St. Laurence's life of prayer,
wise leadership and love
for humanity, inspire us
to live our lives in truth,
love and service as he did.

Psalm 84, Eph 4:1 -24

7. St. Kevin's Well

Bring your water jar and sit empty
Of all save thirst
And silence

[Marie-Therese Porter]

St. Kevin's Well

Returning back through the wood from St. Saviour's monastery on to the Green Road an old cottage comes into view. This is the only house on that side of the road all the way to the upper lake. A large family lived there until fairly recent times. Seeing the house might evoke thoughts of home. Do you see yourself as part of the larger family on earth?

St. Kevin's well is located between the river and the road within sight of the old monastery of Glendalough. It is one hundred and fifty meters east of the bridge that crosses the river to the Visitor's Centre. The well is easy to miss except that a mound of earth surrounds it and a birch tree grows near the opening of the entrance path. That tree is recognisable because of pieces of cloth and mementoes left hanging on it by pilgrims. This continues a tradition of leaving an intention or request behind in memory of the visit to a holy well. We all like to be remembered.

A Source of Life

Not so long ago wells were the only source of clean water for Irish country people. As a result they were well protected and regularly cleaned. In ancient times wells were regarded as entrances to the womb of the earth and believed to be under the protection of feminine guardian spirits. Indeed many of the great rivers of Ireland including the Boyne, the Erne and the Shannon are called after goddess spirits who protected their sources. When Christianity came to Ireland, some of the old beliefs and sacred places were adapted and inserted into the new religion. For example, Brigit, the ancient goddess, appeared in the new form of Brigid, the Christian saint. Many holy wells throughout the country are called after her.

One of the most beautiful things about a well is its stillness. Its source is from below, where the water enters quietly, never disturbing the surface. When a well is clear it is like a mirror showing a perfect reflection. Looking into it is like looking into a great eye. What do you see as you look into the water? Can you see your own reflection? Do your looks reflect how you feel inside? Be aware of what your appearance says about you – where you have come from, the choices you have made, the difficulties and disappointments you have endured, the ambitions you have realised, the dreams you still hold for yourself. View these things not with judgement but with affection and admiration, for they make you the person you are in God's eyes.

Water is an essential element of life because nothing survives without it. There is an old custom in Ireland of keeping holy water in the house and using it constantly for blessing and protection. People love to walk beside rivers and along the seashore. It is said that the sounds of moving water attract us because they remind us of the very first sounds that we heard as babies in our mother's womb. Sitting beside the still waters of a well can help put us in touch with the source of life deep within us from which spring hopes and desires. *Do you have a sense of your life flowing from the very heart of your being?*

During the course of the summer months in recent years St. Kevin's well has dried up completely. Older local people say that never happened in the past. They remember that even in the hottest days of summer it was always full of the coolest water. Perhaps the deep source of the well has dried up for some reason making it now depend solely on surface water. Wells also need to be cleaned from time to time, otherwise they tend to quickly fill up with dead, useless matter. We too need to attend to our inner well, which can so easily become cluttered with our worldly concerns.

In the past, many wells were regarded as having healing properties for various ills including diseases of the eyes. Nowadays doctors take care of our eye problems but who cares for the inner eye? Dip your hands deep into the well, symbolising your desire to live with depth, clarity and vision. Bring the water with your two hands to your forehead, touching that place between your eyes where your inner eye is located. Cross your hands over your heart. Finally face the palms of your hands towards the earth, with awareness that you are seeking a harmony of body, mind and spirit. Ask for blessing and good health in the name of the Triune God saying the words, 'May God bless me, may St. Kevin bless me and I bless myself in the name of the Father, Son and Holy Spirit.'

Biblical and Christian Connections

It is quite disconcerting to search for the well and find it empty. Nobody likes to find emptiness where they expect fullness. The biblical story of Hagar in the desert is a very moving one. Abraham rejected her because of the jealousy of his wife Sarah. In her darkest moment she discovered that there was a well in the desert close to where she lay with her son preparing for death. (Genesis 21:19) *What is your experience of broken dreams and sources of inspiration drying up?*

There are many Biblical stories that tell of wells as meeting places where important relationships began. Isaac was introduced to Rebekah at a well (Genesis 24) and Moses met Zipporah (Exodus 2:15-22). It is a reminder that while our physical thirst has to be satisfied, we also need significant relationships. Probably the best-known story of all concerns Jesus and the Samaritan woman (John 4:6-30). They were strangers when they met but offered each other unconditional companionship, kindness and understanding. Do you believe you can meet the Lord at the well and enter into conversation with Him without fear of being judged or condemned? *Do you leave others with the feeling they have been heard and understood?*

When St. Patrick came to Ireland, we are told that he baptized some of the first Christians at the ancient wells. Resting beside the well is a good place to recall our own initiation into the Christian community. When we were small children our parents and sponsors brought us to the church where water was poured over us in the Sacrament of Baptism. As an adult in the present time, what does it mean to be a part of the Christian family? *Are your immediate family all that matters to you now? How is God asking you to live?*

The Voice of the River

As you prepare to depart from St. Kevin's Well, you may feel drawn to the Glendasan River that flows nearby. You will notice it contains still, deep pools alongside chattering racy shallows. Large granite stones lie in the bed of the river to the left but they do not impede the continuous flow of the water. They only bring about changes in direction which adds to the variety and sound of the river's movement. *What effect do the obstacles that stand in your path have on the direction and flow of your life?*

These are questions you might ponder as you set out again on your journey back along the riverbank towards the bridge.

Go mbeannaí Dia duit,
a Chaoimhín Naofa,
Go mbeannaí Muire duit,
agus beannáim féin duit,
Is chugatsa a tháinig mé ag
Gearrán mo phéin duit,
Is ag iarraidh carthanachta
ar son Dé.

May God bless you, St. Kevin,
May Mary bless you, and I bless
you myself. To yourself I have come to
complain of my problems
And to ask your charity for
God's sake

[Old Irish Prayer said at Holy wells]

Psalm 42
John 3: 13-17

44

8. The Monastic City

Bell tower muted,
cloister cold and stark.
Shrouded in stillness,
ghostly grey stones
breathe out the
prayers of centuries

[Bernadette Knopek] ·

The Round Tower

Monastic Living before the 12th Century

At a point in the landscape where rivers and valleys come together, the monastic city of Glendalough was established and flourished from the sixth century onwards. The model for the old monastery was that of a circle within a circle. These were joined at the Gateway from which a passage led directly to the heart of the monastery where the cathedral church and the burial ground for the dead were located. Also situated within the inner circle were the abbot's house, the round tower, the refectory and houses to accommodate guests. It is noteworthy that the guests included refugees as well as pilgrims, all of whom were given a place at the very heart of the monastic enclosure.

The outer circle enclosed a large area covering many acres of ground within which a community of several hundred people lived. The monks formed the core of the group and their prayer, work and study were at the heart of monastic life. All the activities of an early Irish monastery would have taken place here, including writing, illumination of manuscripts, agriculture, metalwork, tanning and many other crafts. Buildings would have probably included the bakery, kitchen, infirmary, refectory, scriptorium and library. Students stayed in the monastery for a longer or shorter time receiving tutorial education from various masters. Families, including women and children, were also resident and some of the monks were lay people. Life was lived throughout the monastery with a total commitment to the spiritual and temporal needs of a living, working community. There would have always been a listening ear to share setbacks and life's tragedies and an understanding that most healing takes place in the give and take of relationships. This was a very different model of monastic life from the more exclusive form introduced by the Augustinians at St. Saviour's church.

Life in the early monasteries was based on living the Gospels. We know from the few surviving books of Rules that the primary purpose of the monk was to follow Christ. Details concerning daily life took second place to that. Study was based on the Scriptures and the foundations of faith and its application came from that source. The monasteries became centres of learning and it was from there that the mission of the Celtic church developed. Bishops resided in the monasteries but their purpose was mainly liturgical. The Abbot was the administrator and head of the community.

The monastic city is known locally to this day as the Seven Churches. Many of these churches were quite small and situated within the outer circle of the settlement. Specific groups most likely used them as chapels for prayer and reflection. The whole community would come together in the cathedral for Sunday worship and at various times during the day for the Office prayers. It was a model of small Christian groups operating within a larger network that might be relevant again in our time.

Standing on the Threshold

The best way to enter the monastic city is through the Gateway, which was the threshold into the sanctuary. It is good to pause and look through the archways towards the ruins of the cathedral inside. Be aware that you are about to enter a passage through time and space. In Celtic tradition the way into a sacred place was always marked by a passage, bringing together the sacred and the secular, the inner and outer worlds, the individual and the community. It emphasized the links between all of these and gave a person entering an opportunity to make those connections.

Just inside the gate, on the wall on the right hand side of the passage, there is a great slab of mica schist with a cross incised on it. This is known as the sanctuary cross. Enter the passage slowly, thinking of the links you want to make. Be mindful of the refugees who seek sanctuary today in many countries including Ireland. *Do they receive the hospitality and security that was always extended to the stranger in Irish Christian tradition?*

A Beacon of Imagination and Faith

Inside the inner circle of the monastery the Round Tower stands guard over the ancient ruins. This splendid structure has survived for over a thousand years. It is a memorial to the imagination and determination of the people who built it and a powerful expression of life, endurance and faith, with its seven storeys possibly symbolising the seven stages of life itself. We are told that the round towers were built to protect the treasures of the monastery when raiders came to steal them. *What is your special treasure and how do you protect it? How does your life stand witness to what you believe?*

Surrounding the round tower and the main church there are many gravestones. Some are ancient, others quite recent. It was an Irish custom to bury the dead beside the church so that when people came to pray they visited the dead and felt united with them in spirit. The inscriptions speak of lives lived, of the sad loss of young people and the love felt by those left behind. Cemeteries are always a reminder of how brief and fragile even the longest life is. It makes one realise how important it is to live each day as fully as we can and how often we fail to do that.

Echoes of Prayer and Worship

The stones of the cathedral church hold memories of prayer and worship offered to God by night and day throughout the centuries. The monks prayed the Office Hours in common at various times during the day and led the weekly Sunday worship. They were also responsible for the night vigils, which continued throughout the hours of darkness when the majority of the community were asleep.

Cathedral doorway

The large flagstones in the lower part of the walls may have come from the first stone church built on this site which replaced the original wooden churches. The decorated archway, fragments of which still remain, was inserted in the twelfth century at the same time as St. Saviour's monastery was built. Stand for a while in silence catching the echoes coming from this sacred place. Would you like to add your voice? *For what would you like to give thanks at this moment?*

St. Kevin's Cross and Church

South of the door of the cathedral stands St. Kevin's cross. The Celtic cross is a treasure of the Irish spiritual tradition and is unique in that the arms and shaft are connected together in a circle. Esther de Waal in her book *A World Made Whole* [Fount Books 1991], notes that old Irish spirituality was creation-filled but cross-centred, and she sees in the Celtic cross "the circle of creation held in tension with the cross of redemption". For Celtic Christians the experience of God's presence was sensed in nature but even more so in the idea of Christ carrying his cross on behalf of humanity. Those who followed Christ expected to take up their cross daily and travel with Him.

Our world is full of crosses. Most of us carry a cross at some time in our life and feel its weight upon our shoulders.

Sometimes it can mark our progress to a new experience of life and the darkest and most difficult moments in our lives often bring out the best in us. *What crosses do you bear and how do you carry them?* There are also communal crosses. The strength of Irish people's faith through centuries of suffering came from their belief that Christ's suffering on their behalf was greater than their own. An important part of Christian mission is helping others carry their cross.

St. Kevin's Cross

There is a custom of making a wish while embracing St.Kevin's Cross. Why not make time to do this before leaving the Monastic City? *What are your wishes for yourself and humanity at large and how do you hope to make them come true?*
Near the cathedral stands St. Kevin's Church which is unusual in that it is a church and round tower combined. It is beautifully preserved and the best-known monument in Glendalough along with the round tower. It is fitting that this church has survived better than the other churches because it is a monument to the memory of St. Kevin which is still alive after fourteen hundred years.

Soul Friendship

Come and share the freshness of your soul,
That which frees and does not bind,
That each may walk the earth anew,
And blossom forth to nature's way.

[Shadows: Sean Hogan]

Across from St. Kevin's Church lie the ruins of St. Kieran's Church. The monks at Glendalough probably dedicated this church to St. Kieran of Clonmacnoise because Kevin and Kieran were contemporaries and friends. In ancient Ireland there was a tradition of friendship known as *anamchairdeas* [soul friendship]. This special kind of companioning developed amongst the early desert Christian hermits in Egypt, Syria and Palestine. They chose to live in solitude but also became famous for the depth of friendship, care and mentoring they offered those seeking their help and guidance. It was as if their love of being alone was not an obstacle to intimate friendship but a prerequisite for it.
This tradition eventually became embodied in the Sacrament of Confession in the western Christian church, but

in the early days of Christianity in Ireland anyone [lay or cleric, man or woman] acting as a teacher, confessor or spiritual guide would be referred to as an *anamchara*. This special relationship implied a reciprocal intimacy, trust and interdependence. Recorded in the ninth century is a story where St. Brigid of Kildare counsels a young cleric to find a soul friend "for anyone without a soul friend is like a body without a head". *[Martyrology of Oengus the Culdee:* Whitley Stokes: ed]

Soul friends shared a deep love for one another with respect for each other's wisdom. Their relationship was honest, affirming and compassionate but also very challenging at times. They would mentor each other, and understood that God is close to those who speak heart to heart, as friends do. The main purpose of the friendship however, was to encourage one another to live in imitation of Jesus through penance, prayer and a change of heart.

Today we live in a highly mobile and increasingly anonymous world where we are inclined to make 'contacts' rather than friends. This can increase our feelings of loneliness. *How do you experience friendship in your life? What are your expectations of those close to you, and what expectations do you allow them to have of you?*

Lord,
Help me to be a loyal, loving
and trusting friend.
To understand that the
friendship I offer
Is an expression
of your love for us.

Psalm 134
John 15: 1-17

9. The Road to the Desert

Footsteps halt
Beside lake waters silent and brown.
A stillness more than silence
Echoes in my soul
Tuned to the Ultimate Sound.

[Bernadette Knopek]

The Lower Lake

The Road Inwards

Leaving the monastic city through the exit near St.Kevin's Church a wooden bridge crosses over the river that flows from the lakes. Overhanging trees and bushes amplify every sound and movement from the water below. Nearby, there is a cluster of granite stones including one with a hollow in the centre. This is a bullaun that was used in the past for grinding corn and herbs and is known as the Deer Stone. There is a story that a baby was left in St. Kevin's care and protection. Having no way of sustaining the child he prayed for assistance which came in the form of a doe leaving milk in the stone every day. It is a beautiful and tender story of harmonious dependence between people and animals.

The road from the monastic city to St. Kevin's hermitage near the upper lake is a continuation of what is popularly known as the Green road, the nature part of which we have already explored. As you walk the road here the emphasis will be on making a transition from community to a place of solitude. The path passes through the dark side of the valley where for many months of the year the sun never shines. Its destination is a place called in Irish, 'Diseart Chaoimhín' (Kevin's Desert). Become aware as you walk of all the thousands of pilgrims who have walked this way in soul-searching and prayer. Their spirits invite us to do the same today.

The Monster In the Lake

Half way between the old monastery and the hermitage, there is a small lake called Loch na Peiste. Legend records that a monster lived in this lake and Kevin came face to face with it on his journey to the desert. His response was unusual in that instead of avoiding or destroying the monster he befriended it and took it with him. This is a key story. Kevin made the dramatic choice as a young man to live in isolation under extremely harsh conditions. He could not have done this unless he was aware of his strengths while confronting and befriending his own inner contradictions. His decision to take the monster with him was a moment of enlightenment that transformed the lake into a place of healing.

Stories and their Meaning

Stories are a powerful way to communicate important truths. The story about Kevin and the monster is not about an actual creature in the lake but about the importance of facing the truth of who he really was. It has been said that monster stories in all traditions are an attempt by humanity to look at its own inner face. Life itself can hurt us in so many ways and as a result there are uneasy secrets buried deep inside all of us. Loss, betrayal, disappointments and resentment often leave us frustrated, guilty and angry. Sometimes we even hold onto our hurts as a way of keeping power in a situation. Most of us are in need of healing but we all know how difficult it is to be compassionate and forgiving toward the undesirable parts of others and ourselves. Furthermore, when life deals us cruel and unexpected blows we find ourselves crying out in anger 'Why does God let this happen?' There are no easy answers to this question. Perhaps the best we can do in those situations is to sit patiently with open, empty hands.

When we live in community or family, we may try to deal with our inner demons by projecting them on to others. However, when we choose to be alone we cannot do this so easily. If we want to enter a place of solitude within ourselves, even for a limited time, we must be prepared to accept ourselves totally, demons and all. The prophet Isaiah expressed this paradox beautifully – 'Wolves and sheep will live together in peace, and leopards will lie down with young goats.

Calves and lion cubs will feed together, and little children will take care of them' [Is 11:6]

On the shores of Loch na Peiste a few years ago a visitor recounted a vivid dream she once had. She and a group of people were standing by a lake wanting to cross to the other side. A huge creature that filled the water from shore to shore occupied the lake. Since it was very still as if asleep they decided to walk across its back one by one, slowly and quietly. All the others got across safely but she was last in line and before she got to the other side the creature moved and plunged her into the water. When a large tentacle was wrapped around her waist and then around her neck she was terrified, and thought her last moment had come. After a while she realised the creature was not trying to drown her but rescue her. This dream illustrates how even our worst fear can be our salvation if only we see it in a new way.

The Healing of Hurts

The pilgrim road to the lower lake,
the little lake of healing –
touch, wash your wounds, and so forsake
your need of their concealing.

[Roger Hickley]

On the road to the desert of Glendalough there will be little appreciation of what lies ahead unless you spend some time by the lake tenderly acknowledging the painful parts of your own story. In the past, when pilgrims came to this lake they sought the blessing of its waters. Find a suitable place to sit quietly on the shore. Go to the lake and fill the cup of your hands with the cold water. Let this represent the distress you want to expose and address. Allow the water to trickle through your fingers back into the lake. Try to let your pain diminish as each drop escapes your grasp. Fill your hands again and while bathing your face, pray for the gift of facing the road ahead with new eyes. When old wounds are healed we are freer to respond to life rather than react against it.

The Blessing of Winter

In Glendalough during the winter months silence deepens in the valley. The daytime sun seldom breaks through the gloomy mist. The rivers and lakes ebb and flow with the comings and goings of the rain. The deer descend from the mountains in search of food and the oak trees by the Green Road stand strong and still holding the promise of another springtime.

In cold weather the dark side of the valley stays frozen even when the sun shines brightly on the other side of the lake. Standing on the southern lakeshore you are facing north, the direction of winter. The spiritual gift of this season is dormancy, emptiness, letting go. Take time to remember the winter times of your life when bleak bitter winds blew into the face of your dreams and aspirations. Think of empty times when you had to let go against your wishes and times when you felt frozen and unable to move in any direction. Winter is also a time when new life is forming just below the surface. Become aware of quiet places within yourself and of new seeds of life that are waiting to be born. *What new life would you like to find?*

Images from Nature as Guide

As you travel along the road let images of nature be your guide. On bright, still days the lake is like a mirror with the world above reflected below. This could be an image of the ability we have as human beings to reflect on all we see. The human being is designed to stand and wonder. Why did God endow us with this supreme gift of consciousness? It is the fountain and source of our imagination and creativity, but also our contradictions. Is it God's way of entrusting us with an appreciation of all creation?

Watch out for an upside-down tree that fell but grew again because some of its roots remained fixed in the ground. A large granite rock with a broken piece at its base lies at the foot of a tall oak tree. Once upon a time an acorn fell into a crack in this rock and as the tree grew it split the stone open. It was as if the rock's heart had to be broken open in order for new life and growth to occur. *Could that be true of us too?*

Further along a gentle stream from the mountain becomes a little waterfall as it approaches the road. The breeze through the nearby birch trees and the sound of the water falling softly might be a reminder of life's sighs and tears. There is a contemplative atmosphere in this ancient woodland. The birch is the oldest native Irish tree and is also known as the lady of the forest. These groves can put us in touch with a feminine expression of God. The forest floor is carpeted with beautiful mosses and other special vegetation. Walk softly among these trees. You too are part of nature's dream.

Almighty, ever-loving God,
You walk with me as I
carry the burden
Of my hurts and
disappointments.
Help me understand
the blessing
They can bring me.
Touch my wounds with
your loving hand.

Psalm 23
Mark 5: 21 - 43

Birch Trees

10. The Desert of St. Kevin

Above reflection the rounded cave invites.
Bone-rock bed of the austere saint.
Access requires a wild path,
A cold drench to trouble the upheld image;
Demands a difficult climb.
Achieved is no place of bodily comfort
But where to observe and be silent.
A socket for a motionless eye to see itself
As mist and mind admit pervasive light,
And through a diffused sun perceive a presence
Touched lightly and still beyond grasping.

[Richard Hills]

Inside St. Kevin's Bed

On the southern shore of the upper lake in Glendalough, the desert of Kevin is situated. It is difficult to understand why this area is called a desert because the first impression is of a well-watered place with a crystal-clear stream flowing down from the mountain and magnificent oak trees growing beside it. Water, racing in the river and breaking gently along the shore of the lake creates a harmonious background sound. Above the southern shore of the lake the hills rise steeply from the water. There is a feeling here that it is a meeting place of earth and heaven. The invitation to linger for a while savouring the presence of the real and the mysterious is very strong. A seat on the lakeshore encourages sitting and thinking or simply sitting.

Early Irish Christianity was influenced by pre-Christian Celtic religion which was fundamentally positive in its understanding of the world. It therefore lacked a sense of sin or divine punishment. The spirit world was felt in and through the natural world. Evil and its effects were an ever-present reality but there was a belief that good always prevailed. Life was understood to be an heroic journey lived with the hope of reaching an eternal place of youth, rest and freedom from sorrow known as Tir na nÓg. Courage and bravery were seen as essential qualities on this epic journey. Christianity adapted many of these fundamental beliefs and only changed them gradually.

The Desert and Eremitic Spiritual Tradition

The desert experience has deep roots in Christianity. John the Baptist, who announced to the people of Israel the coming of Christ, preached prayer and penance as the way to prepare for Him. He led by example spending many years as an ascetic in the desert, eating locusts and wild honey [Mt 3]. Jesus Himself, before he began his public ministry, spent forty days in the desert of Judea. He was tempted several times to abandon the experience but he persevered and emerged with a clear understanding of His core message and how he wanted to put it into practice. This was expressed in the Sermon on the Mount (Mt. Chaps 5,6 and 7) and remains at the heart of Christian teaching.

View of St. Kevin's Bed from across the lake

The desert spiritual tradition came to Ireland from the East where St. Anthony of Egypt became the first hermit. He retired alone into the harsh desert and lived his life with great austerity in search of God. The heroic nature of this approach appealed to the instincts and imagination of the Irish Celts whose mythical heroes were well known for their deeds of bravery and physical endurance. The hermit experience was introduced to Ireland by Patrick and quickly became an established part of early Irish Christianity. Mystics like Kevin believed that Christ would be a strict judge of their commitment and discipleship but also their greatest source of companionship and hope. They found their deserts in isolated places among rocks in the mountains or in caves and cliffs beside lakes and the sea. The extreme element in such places was probably the winter cold which must have been almost unbearable.

The hermit experience was a radical option to live in solitude in some out of the way place. It was a penitential and ascetic choice, the purpose of which was to liberate the person entirely from earthly attractions in order to serve God more completely. The early Celtic Christians acknowledged a sense of sinfulness and a need for redemption. They accepted a strong emphasis on penance and metanoia [change of heart].

There can be no doubt that the call of the desert was a genuine calling but its extreme expression was open to exaggeration. A negative consequence of this severe self-discipline was a dualistic approach that became part of Irish Christianity. The body came to be regarded as a necessary evil, endangering the salvation of the immortal soul. Christian spirituality became centred on suffering and a God who willed suffering as the way to salvation. *How do you channel your passions and deepest desires?*

St. Kevin's Bed and Teampall na Skellig

This place belongs to him,
He said, and others like him
We are strangers here
Until we make
The inner journey
Home to ourselves

[Marian O'Sullivan]

On the remote shore of the upper lake in Glendalough Kevin established a small monastery and lived out the call of the desert. On the cliff face nearby he found a small womb-like cave in the rocks. This

Teampall na Skellig

ancient Bronze Age tomb is a reminder of how from the earliest times human beings had a need to express their understanding of the mystery of death and the afterlife. Like all hermits Kevin chose hardship quite deliberately. In this lonely place he would have been tested to the limit of his endurance, but perhaps discovered the poetry of his own soul.

In the past a visit to St. Kevin's Bed marked the high point of the Glendalough pilgrimage. After crossing by boat to Teampall na Skellig pilgrims would disembark on the lakeshore and climb rough steps hewn in the rock until they came to a wide cleft in the cliff known as the Chair. There they would gather quietly until it was their turn to be lowered down one by one into the cave. This was quite dangerous as there is a vertical drop of ten metres from the entrance of the cave down into the lake. However, many people were prepared to risk it, including women, because it was believed that one of the blessings attached to visiting St. Kevin's Bed was protection for women during pregnancy and a safe delivery in childbirth.

Nowadays it is strongly advised that people do not go unaccompanied to the heart of St. Kevin's Desert because the path is very rugged and dangerous. It is a journey to an edge that is unreachable for most people. Along the Miner's Road on the opposite side of the lake there are many good viewing points to both these places. From there it is possible to see clearly that St. Kevin's Bed and Teampall na Skellig are situated at a meeting point where the horizontal lake meets the vertical cliffs. Our own journey to God is a here and now experience that always brings us to a point of reaching out to something above and beyond us.

If you call aloud from the opposite shore in the direction of St. Kevin's Bed a clear echo of your own voice comes back. It is a reminder that we need to listen to the questions we ask, as the answers may well be within us. Find a rock on which to sit and contemplate the meaning of the desert experience, and accept the feeling of something just out of reach. *What is your experience of desert in your life? How do you fulfil your dreams, or are they always beyond your grasp?*

Fadaigh inár gcroíte, a
Thíarna, solas an chreidimh,
Lasair an dóchais,
Agus tine an ghrá

Kindle in our hearts, O Lord,
The light of faith,
the flame of hope
and the fire of love.

[Sr. Colmcille Connolly]

Psalm 40, 1 Kings 19: 9 ff

11. St. Kevin's Cell

Silence is budding time
Solitude full flower
The harvest, serenity.
The only time is Now
This moment of Eternity

[Bernadette Knopek]

Site of St. Kevin's Cell

Since it is not possible to visit the heart of the Glendalough desert around St. Kevin's Bed, it is good to spend some time in the next most important part of the hermitage around St. Kevin's Cell. There is no doubt the saint lived and prayed for a time there in comparative solitude. From near Reefert church, follow signs pointing to a ledge and then take the path leading to steps wending their way up the steep slope to the site. Ascending the flights of steps is a reminder of the flight of the years and all the steps we have travelled.

All that is left of the old cell now are a few precious foundation stones with three oak trees growing up around them like three strong spirits protecting the place. This was once a hut built with dry stone walls, circular in shape, twelve feet in diameter and no more than eleven feet high. It sloped inwards gradually in the shape of a traditional beehive. Within this dwelling the hermit lived and prayed in accordance with the well-known principle of the desert tradition: "Go sit in your cell and your cell will teach you everything". There is a stillness about this place that encourages listening with the heart. At these times it is possible that we may hear the voice of God speaking within us. *What is your image of God?*

Prayer of The Heart

May you be blessed, Lord
For all you are
For all your creatures
Your beautiful world
And for giving me this moment
To praise you.

[A pilgrim in Glendalough]

Beehive Hut

What does praying actually imply? Is it the way we express our longing for unity and wholeness? Too often we might see prayer as a matter of words, of asking for things, almost bargaining with God. However, the fact that we pray at all suggests we have an innate appreciation of the mystery of the divine and long for its kindly intervention. There are times when it is appropriate to give voice to our concerns, but perhaps prayer is first and foremost an invitation to be present to the here and now. Contemplative prayer has been described as a long, loving look at the real. This requires a quiet and empty mind. Paul Murray has expressed it well in his poem *Living Life to the Full* – 'When your heart is empty / and your hands are empty / you can take into your hands the gift of the present. You can experience in your heart / the moment in all its fullness.' [*The Absent Fountain:* Daedalus Press 1991]. *How and why do you pray?*

Ideally prayer is an experience of being alone with God. What is the difference between solitude and loneliness? Loneliness can be described as being dejected at being alone. It implies finding oneself apart by circumstance rather than by choice. Most of us are afraid of being lonely and fear we do not have the inner resources to cope.   Solitude on the other hand is very much an active decision to move to some kind of individual seclusion, usually with an aim or intention in mind. It suggests we have confidence in our ability to be away from our usual support structures and are prepared to be open to the unexpected. The heart of solitude is not isolation but communion.

St.Kevin and The Blackbird

There is a beautiful story of St. Kevin and a blackbird where the bird came and laid an egg in the saint's outstretched hand. We can imagine Kevin holding his hand and heart open until the process of life giving was complete. It is a very tender image and suggests that while prayer is experienced in the heart it is put into practice through willing and open hands. The poet Seamus Heaney reflects how in that moment Kevin "found himself linked into the network of eternal life and was moved with pity" [*The Spirit Level.* Faber 1996]. Imogen Stuart's granite sculpture expresses this story in another form. You will find it situated at the top of the steps on the slope above St. Kevin's cell. It is a permanent and evocative reminder of stillness and gentle relationship. As people pass the sculpture they often caress the shape and form of the bird. How often we ignore our sense of touch as a way of being touched by what we see.

The Net of Indra

Spend time sitting in St. Kevin's Cell holding in your heart the wonder and interconnectedness of all things. In Buddhist-Hindu tradition there is a metaphorical understanding of the net of the goddess Indra. At each link of the net there is a jewel. Each jewel in turn, owes its existence to and reflects every other jewel in the net. Nothing exists alone or in isolation. This is a lovely image of the living universe. Whatever happens to one life form causes a shimmer throughout the entire web of life. Every person and every thing on this earth and in the whole of creation forms one precious web of existence.

Stillness and Listening

People dream of a special experience of God at St. Kevin's Cell but often find their best intentions distracted by the marauding midges that are more interested in blood than prayer. At these times it is sensible to move away from the source of discomfort. Actually, most of us find it hard to sit quietly for more than a few moments even in the best of conditions. People are curious as to how Kevin coped with the uncomfortable realities of life in the woods, but perhaps the real question to ask is, *how do I deal with distractions and irritations in my life?*

Providing the midges are not tormenting you, sit still on one of the foundation stones or rest against one of the oak trees. Be aware of the sights and sounds all around. Breathe in deeply the freshness and purity of the air. Be aware of how you are feeling. What is your body saying to you? Are you aware of your emotions? What are the thoughts running through your mind? Listen carefully for a while and honour all your thoughts and feelings.

Enter more consciously into the rhythm of deep breathing. In your imagination move inwards and focus on that spark of pure light and life that God has placed deep in your heart. Name and claim this pure light within you as your gifts and talents, and everything else that makes you a unique person in God's creation. Become aware that God's presence is as close to you as your inner self. Rest in the silence for as long as you wish. Slowly bring your awareness back to the sights and sounds all around you. You may find that your sight is clearer and your ear more finely tuned to what you hear.

Ever-living, ever-loving God
Grant me a listening ear,
A seeing eye,
A still body
And a loving heart.

Psalm 139
Matt 4: 1-11

St. Kevin and the Blackbird
Sculpture: Imogen Stuart

12. Reefert Church

He calls me to the lonely place
In town or far apart
With Him I die and live again
Right here within my heart.

[Eileen Gallagher]

Reefert Church

A Place of Resurrection

The ancient church of Reefert was built within the hermitage of Glendalough and it can safely be assumed that it was St. Kevin's final resting place. After his death, pilgrims would have come to pay their respects and seek favours at his grave and would have needed the support of a resident community during their stay. More recently, local chieftains of the O'Toole clan were buried around the church confirming the fact that this was regarded as the most important burial ground in their territory. The word Reefert means burial place of the kings. For our reflections we refer to it as the church of resurrection.

It is a peaceful place of indigenous oak, birch and hazel trees within an environment that hasn't changed much since Kevin knew it in the sixth century. Situated under the shadow of the high hill of Lugduff, it is dark and cold in winter but completely transformed in summer when the sunlight comes streaming through the trees. During a visit to Reefert, it is almost impossible not to be mindful of life and death, the ancient past and how we are all part of an ongoing story.

The presence of the supernatural in all that exists was characteristic of the old Celtic religions. Within everything lay depths of secrets and mysteries and what seemed solid and impermeable could suddenly change. Many traditional religions including the pagan Celtic believed in life after death as a continuation of this present life. The Christian church inherited this belief in the immortality of the soul. It is not surprising therefore that faith in the resurrection of the Lord and their own resurrection came naturally to these early Christians. They believed that all of life was a search for contentment, and when it was found one would be ready to die. This stage was always referred to as the place of resurrection. Every detail of life was regarded as an important step on this journey.

Can this ancient wisdom teach us something today? Could it simply mean to reach a stage of self-knowledge where we have the courage to be truly ourselves in all we do? Perhaps most of all it is believing that we are beloved on this earth. What does that mean? In western culture we are encouraged to define our worth through performance and comparison with others. We also get caught trying to satisfy others expectations of us. This creates a lot of anxiety and we tend to measure ourselves by asking 'Am I good enough? Am I worth loving?' It is the same with failure. Our society is structured around winners and losers but who is to say what is success or failure? It is hard to believe that just by being alive we are beloved. God offers us all the gifts of life and does not compare or judge us. We are His children, and as parents rejoice in their beloved young so God rejoices in each one of us.

It is a strange paradox that when we accept death and other kinds of loss we can gain a freedom that brings with it new

The Breasal Grave Slab

creativity. In letting go of things we are invited to embrace a greater trust. We are asked only to respond to life with all our heart and soul in the knowledge that we have a place in the wider scheme of things. We are not insignificant and each one of us has a contribution to make.

Do you believe you are beloved on this earth?

Remembering our Dead

Inside the roofless church the old walls are a reminder of beginnings and foundations but also the fact that even great things pass away and die. The space inside is confined and tomb-like which only emphasises the open roof, the hills and sky, and the clouds drifting overhead. In this quiet place take some time to remember the souls of those you have loved who have died. They live on in our memories of special times and all we have shared together. They are our saints and from their place in heaven they can lead and guide us. The month of November, the beginning of the Celtic New Year, is traditionally called the month of the Holy Souls. *Who are you praying for? How would you like to be remembered? Do you take the time for soulful experience?*

Continue to rest around Reefert Church for a while enjoying the gift of being alive. Moving on eventually, there are many special places to visit, along the pathways through the woods and around the lakeshore. Inevitably the call of the surrounding hills may prove irresistible.

Go dtuga Dia an bheatha Shíoraí dá bfuil imithe ar Shlí na fírinne

May God give life eternal to those who have gone on the way of truth

[Old Irish Prayer]

Psalm 90
Wisdom 3:1-9

Cross at Reefert

13. A Walk in The Hills

Camaderry, Lugduff, and Derrybawn,
Towering hills above the darkening lakes,
Sensitive to sunlight or overhanging cloud.
Harsh cry of the raven
Echoing from hill to hill.
What troubles you, dark bird?
Like Kevin in his desert cave, struggling,
Praying and searching for his God.

[Marie Connolly]

View from Lugduff Spink

74

Poulanass Waterfall

Above St. Kevin's Cell the forestry road leads upward through the woodland to the hills beyond. Most of us love to climb into the hills to get a better view. On the way up the sound of Poulanass waterfall is an irresistible call. Walkers like to stop for a while at the viewpoint to be refreshed and energized by its constant flow and movement. The water tumbling down can be seen as an image of the hectic rush of life today. The plunge pool below the waterfall slows the speed of the flow for a moment, and is a reminder of the need to wind down and rest. We all need tranquil places to survive the constant and insistent demands that are part of modern living. Some visitors comment that the sound and energy of the pouring water helps them sense the generosity and power of God.

For those who are interested in geography, Poulanass is an example of a hanging valley dating back to the last Ice Age, which ended more than ten thousand years ago. When the river first flowed, it found its way through a natural fault in the old rock. It is consoling to know that God's grace, like the river, flows through the natural cracks and weaknesses that are part of all our lives. The waters of this river are refreshingly bright and clear but very soon they will be absorbed into the dark waters of the lake.

Climbing the Spink

Above the waterfall, the road leads on to a divergence of tracks. The first track on the right leads to a pathway laid with wooden railway sleepers, which climbs through a thousand steps to the summit of Lugduff Spink [follow the white arrow on the signpost]. There are magnificent views of the valley and lakes and the surrounding countryside all along the high part of this pathway. Reaching the heights is demanding on the body but very satisfying for the soul. Things that look quite formidable at ground level look insignificant from above. Is that because we feel freer in ourselves when we have a broader view?

The fresh air blowing over high ground is exhilarating and encourages a sense of wonder at the magnificence of the world in which we live. Many ancient religions believed that their gods lived on mountaintops. Perhaps that is because the tops of mountains seem to reach out and touch heaven. It is not surprising that mystics sought places where the air was pure, the skies were clear and God seemed to be nearer. Moses received the Law on top of Mount Sinai and Jesus experienced Transfiguration on Mount Tabor.

The Price of Progress

After reaching the highest point, the pathway continues downwards towards the end of the valley and crosses the river above the Miner's village. This rugged, beautiful place is damaged by piles of rubble that remain from the mining of lead that took place here in the 19th and 20th centuries. The people who lived in the village at the end of the valley in those days were probably more concerned about keeping body and soul together than the danger of polluting the environment. The most important aspect of the mining story however is that

industrialisation and the rise of capitalism brought so much progress to the world. With greater economic independence ordinary people got a chance for the first time to make choices in their lives and develop a democratic system of government. It is sad, though, that some of the great advances of humanity were made at the huge cost of respect for our environment.

.As we continue to damage the integrity of the earth's natural resources at an alarming rate we threaten our own existence. We are still driving species into extinction and therefore diminishing sources of wonder and beauty that feed our imagination as well as our bodies. Can you imagine a world without a field of wild flowers or the cry of a bird?

Mullacor and the Song of the Lark

A second track above Poulanass goes straight ahead following the river for a while. It eventually joins the Wicklow Way that leads out of the forest on to the moorland and up to the summit of Mullacor, the highest point in these hills. In the moorlands there are many herds of deer. These are timid creatures that blend into the landscape and can easily be missed. The surprising thing is that having seen one you begin to see them all. They are a bit like the soul that is inclined to camouflage itself but once revealed can be found always and in everything. The deer make a sharp warning cry that brings to mind feelings of insecurity and danger. These feelings may be heightened by a sudden change in the weather or by a mist descending to obscure the way.

On the mountains in springtime you are likely to hear the skylark. This little bird lives in the moorlands and makes its nest on the ground, leaving itself very vulnerable and exposed to danger. During the breeding season fear does not prevent it leaving its nest and soaring straight up into the air as far as it can go, pouring out it's heart in joyful song. Its flight and song are like a prayer linking earth and heaven. There is an old Irish poem referring to the lark that is a beautiful evocation of how the natural world turns a person's thoughts toward God:

Learned in music sings the lark
I leave my cell to listen;
His open beak spills music, hark!
Where heavens bright cloudlets glisten.
And so I'll sing my morning psalm
That God bright Heaven may give me,
And keep me in eternal calm
And from all sin relieve me.
[Robin Flower: *The Irish Tradition* [Oxford 1947]

At all times of the year in the mountains it is possible to see and hear the raven, the bird that fed the original desert hermits Anthony and Paul, and also the prophet Elijah in the Old Testament story. The peregrine falcons too, can often be seen in their magnificent flight patrolling their space in the skies over the cliffs above St. Kevin's Bed where they make their nests.

A View from Derrybawn

The third track from Poulanass leads left across the bridge and runs along the brow of Derrybawn hill where there are fine views of the lakes and the site of the Monastic City. This road also leads to a junction with the Wicklow Way. From the high ground take time to look in all directions and then face the south, which is the direction of the high summer sun. The spiritual gift of summer is celebration and creativity. Remember the summers of your life, the times of growth, generosity, fullness, bright colours and warmth. Take pleasure and be contented in who you are today. *What warmth, generosity and light will you offer the future?*

The Wonder of the Universe

Up in the heights the sky is nearer but it is only at night the true wonder of it is revealed. During the hours of darkness, gazing at the Milky Way we cannot comprehend the multitude of stars making up our galaxy, or appreciate that our small planet is floating two-thirds from its centre. It is almost beyond our wildest imagination to understand that the Milky Way galaxy in turn floats in a universe containing at least two billion other galaxies. The ever-changing moon moving across the night sky reminds us that a new day will soon be dawning, and night will then descend elsewhere on the earth. How often do we not even notice the cycles and seasons of life, and how extraordinary they appear when we take the time to stop and be aware.

Is chúgatsa suas, a Dhía,
a chuirim siúl mo chos,
glac mo lámh, labhairt mo
bhéil agus mianta mo chroí,
agus go néiri siad leat féin,
leis an Mac agus leis an
Spiorad Naomh

It is to yourself, O God,
I offer the walking of my foot
the holding of my hand,
the speech of my mouth
and the desires of my heart.
May they give more power to you,
and to your Son
and the Holy Spirit.

[Old Irish Prayer]

Psalm 8, Matt 17: 1 - 8

79

14. The Caher and Lakeshore

The hurried lapping sounds
of water on the shore
Speak of many
of my disturbances.
My inner being seeks
the solitude of the deep,
the calm of peace,
the centre of being,
the spirit of God,
dwelling within.

[Liam Lacey]

The Caher

On the Lakeshore

After descending the hills and before departing from the hermitage, why not stand for a few moments of reflection at the centre of the shore of the upper lake and recall the many places you have visited within the valley of Glendalough. The waves breaking on the shore bring your journey to a standstill. Looking across at the cliffs along the southern shore of the lake you will realize there are many places that you have not yet seen or explored.

As you stand there in silence, on occasions you will be aware of children's voices calling one another. They are probably engaged in the excitement of a treasure hunt. We often spend our time searching for treasure outside ourselves. Kevin's life suggests he found the treasure within himself. He chose to be alone in this quiet, remote and beautiful place and his daring became a source of inspiration for the great monastic community that flourished in the valley after his death. His example has challenged many others down the ages to be true to themselves and live life as authentically as possible.

Standing on the lakeshore we are looking toward the west, the direction of autumn and sunset. Autumn's spiritual gift is to harvest memories and glean wisdom, resting in fruitfulness and rich colours and giving thanks for the wealth of our experience. The valley is splendid in autumn, with the vibrant colours reminding us of fulfilment and maturity.

The Wild Geese

A few wild geese have been returning year after year to the lakes. Why do they come to breed in Glendalough when their summer destination is normally Greenland? What happened in the past to bring them here and how has that message been passed down to the next generation? There is a legend that when Kevin first came to Glendalough he approached a local chieftain for a piece of land to develop his hermitage. The ruler had a goose which happened to be sick when Kevin arrived. The goose was very valuable because it brought fish every day for the king's dinner. He promised Kevin that he would give him all the land over which the goose could fly if he would cure it. The saint worked the miracle and so got all the land he needed for his monastery. Whatever the reason for the geese coming back they attract a lot of attention every year. Maybe they represent the longing of our own wild spirit for freedom and flight.

Sometimes we can only stand helplessly by as nature follows her course. A park worker devotedly waited in anticipation this year for the geese to return to the lakes, and was delighted when they arrived back and proceeded to start a new family. They nested on the lower lakeshore near mallards, which are particularly vulnerable to the attention of predators. One morning he discovered that a fox had killed all the geese. 'That's the end of that story' he remarked sadly.

The Caher – An Old Homestead

From the lakeshore it is a short walk to an old circular fort known as the Caher, which stands on open ground in a green field. It is likely that the circular stone wall once surrounded a homestead in medieval or early Christian times. Within this circle the family members lived in their own individual little houses that were made of mud and wattle or wood. The flagstones that can still be seen were probably once the floor of the main building where they all met to share meals and stories.

Long ago there were dense forests everywhere and wild animals were never far away. People lived constantly with danger and sought safety in the security of the homestead. They could not protect themselves in isolation and would turn to each other and to God for help by saying the breastplate prayers. Before beginning to pray they would sometimes make a circle on the ground around them. These prayers were like cloaks drawn around them for safety and reassurance. Pause for a moment within the encircling hills and sense yourself cloaked in God's loving care.

Leaving the Hermitage

Standing in the Caher you will become aware that it is surrounded by hills. There is a feeling of being protected in the valley but also challenged to discover what is beyond the mountains. At the end of the pilgrim walks with groups of people in Glendalough we often stand within the Caher and face the four directions in turn. From the east comes the morning light that breaks through the darkness of the night, the rising sun a symbol of the Risen Christ. The cool refreshing north wind is like the breath of the Spirit that brings the gifts of energy and consciousness. Earth's fruitfulness is enjoyed in the warm south, whilst the west is the source of the rain and home of the setting sun. Having opened ourselves to the blessing of the elements in every direction we stand together in a circle acknowledging the mystery of God from whom all blessings flow. It is truly a circle whose centre is indefinable and whose circumference is everywhere.

Continue to stand in silence at the Caher for a while, aware of the beauty of creation around you. Be thankful for the road of life that you have travelled and all that you have experienced. The memory of your presence will linger here even when you have departed.

Deep peace of the running wave to you
Deep peace of the flowing air to you
Deep peace of the quiet earth to you
Deep peace of the shining light to you
Deep peace of the God of Peace to you

[Iona blessing]

Psalm 121, Matt 14: 13 - 33

15. A Walk to St. Mary's Church

The cliffs and trees and streams you pass,
the sheep in emerald fold,
'He lets me rest in fields of grass'
and sense the Shepherd's hold.

[Roger Hickley]

St. Mary's Church

New Pathway over Old Ground

On the way back to the monastic city it is good to take the new wooden pathway to avoid traffic. This leads along the brighter side of the valley where people express themselves in the way they live, the houses they build and the gardens they cultivate.

Near the beginning of the boardwalk, herds of wild goats that were once domestic are often seen roaming free eating whatever they can find. Further along sheep graze unperturbed in the fields. People often stop to look at these animals. Perhaps the sheep represent our domesticated natures, whilst the goats represent our more instinctual selves. *What expression do you allow your instinctive self?*

From the opposite side of the lake this side looks very attractive, but as you walk along the boardwalk you may be surprised to find that it crosses a marsh in a number of places. A marsh is a self-governing place with many forms of life that are not found elsewhere. Every component has its own part to play and is true to its nature. It has its own natural system of filtering and purifying water for example. Home to many different creatures and plants, throughout the seasons it is possible to witness it's constant and creative self-renewal. It is once again a reminder of the perfection intrinsic to all creation. *What is your true nature? Do you believe it is possible to live creatively and in harmony with the environment?*

Walking along the boards prevents one from sinking into swampy ground in places. Do you ever feel swamped? We all suffer to a certain extent from the multiple roles that we play out in our lives. We are unique individuals, but as human beings we largely define ourselves in relation to others. It may be helpful to ask yourself, *who am I behind all the roles I take up in life?*

St. Mary's – The Church of the Women

Can I allow the feminine in me
To foster new life forms
To nurture the newborn
To care for the fragile
To encourage the spirit that wants to be free?

[Isabelle Smyth]

Along this new pathway to the monastic city, the first church that comes into view is St. Mary's. To find the entrance, it is best to get back onto the main road from the boardwalk. Passing the International hostel, you will come to a sign that points to the church. If you are walking from the monastic city side, it is only a few hundred yards by road away from the gateway of the monastery to a sign pointing to St. Mary's church.

The site is quiet and secluded even though it is only a short distance away from the busiest part of Glendalough. The presence of the feminine is emphasised by the profusion of primroses in spring, followed by bluebells in May. St. Mary's is reputed to be the oldest church in the lower valley, and there is a tradition that it was the burial place of St. Kevin at some stage. It may have been originally at the centre of a community reserved for religious women or simply a church for women as its name in the Irish language suggests (Teampall na mBan).

Due to the difficulty of entering the site, women especially feel some frustration. Is this symbolic of the difficulty women experience in taking their rightful place in many of our institutions? This was not always the case. In the heyday of the monastery, St. Mary's church was part of the wider circle of the community and an integral part of it.

A Doorway Speaks of Many Things

The magnificent doorway of St. Mary's church is constructed with seven great granite stones fitted perfectly together, three on each side and the lintel stone overhead. What did these stones represent in the mind of the designer of the doorway? Could they be the complementary gifts of the masculine and the feminine and the importance of them being acknowledged and appreciated as equally important? The three stones on the right could represent the masculine gifts of ambition, rationality and protection while those on the opposite side might stand for the feminine gifts of intuition, compassion and nurturing. All of these are aspects of the one God. In the Chinese tradition of *yin/yang,* yin is associated with the feminine and yang with the masculine. However, they are not perceived as opposites, but complementary and interdependent - one cannot exist without the other. In the famous yin/yang symbol of the two fishes, *yin* is shown to contain an element of *yang,* and vice-versa.

The symbolism of the doorway is open to many interpretations. Stand on the threshold for a while. Do you have a sense of being a threshold person? *Can you take your place courageously between the past and the future, with respect for the old and openness to the new?* Now stand in the doorway and be aware of both the inner and outer view. This could represent the place where our outer and inner worlds become one. Raising your eyes to the lintel stone, you will see a beautifully carved diagonal saltire cross on the underside of the stone. The cross stretches out to the four corners of the lintel stone with circles in the centre and at the end of the four arms. Through the cross of Christ, circles of reconciliation and unity have been created in every area of life. *How can we contribute to make those circles a reality in our lives?*

Presence of A Gentle Spirit

Inside the church there is a sense of peace and the presence of a gentle spirit. The original building was just one rectangular space with a sanctuary area added later. Maybe the women who lived here designed the church this way. What contribution did women make to Kevin's Monastic City? Some may have been hermits, others teachers and soul-friends. They would have offered a feminine expression of *anamchairdeas* ministry, and may have been particularly active in the area of hospitality to refugees and pilgrims. In Celtic tradition offering welcome was a sacred ministry. It was centred on the mystical belief that any stranger at the door could be a representation of Christ.

Limbo - Burial Place of Stillborn Babies

The first primroses of Spring
I find on the burial plot
of infants we once said
had gone to limbo

What of my unborn dreams?
Can primroses yet blossom
where hopes have died?

[Isabelle Smyth]

Outside the church to the northwest corner of the enclosure there is a small hidden plot marked by rough boundary stones. This is where the bodies of unbaptized babies were buried right up to fairly recent times. It is an abandoned little place which has known the grief and pain of parents who lost their babies before they reached full term. They were offered little sympathy or understanding at the time by a church that created a place outside of heaven called limbo for those children's souls. Many visitors experience a deep sense of loss here. This is also a place to remember our unborn hopes and dreams. Perhaps it is not too late yet for them come to birth.

In the quietness of the grounds of St. Mary's Church it is good to pause for a moment and reflect on the feminine influence in our own lives. This was the women's special place in Glendalough and their memory will always be present here. May the spirits of all the women who ever lived and prayed here give us peace and watch over us on our ongoing journey.

A Mhuire na ngrás,
A Mháthair Mhic Dé,
Go gcuire tú
Ar mo leas mé.

Mary of graces,
Mother of God's Son,
may you set me
on the right course.
[Old Irish Prayer]

Luke 1: 46 – 55: Magnificat
John 12: 1 – 8

Conclusion

No more the frantic stride to reach a destination
But more the ambling pace through the
beauty that surrounds me,
No more the tortured striving to believe in
you, my God,
But more the quiet acceptance of all there
is and will be.
No more the desperate yearning to be
accepted by another
But more the patient, gentle loving of the other.
Can this be the path I'll trod
A path that leads to deep reflection
and resting in the warm embrace of God

[Vera Newport]

Stone crosses where roads meet

Time to Go Home

As you leave Glendalough and begin your journey home you will come to a crossroads where the Wicklow Gap road meets the Laragh to Glendalough road. An old stone with two crosses on it marks their meeting. You probably passed it by without noticing at the beginning of your visit. This is a good place to stand for a little while, reviewing the journey you have just made before moving on into your future. Remember that the end of this pilgrim journey is where you began – another circle has been completed.

Dag Hammarskjold once wrote in his diary 'For all that has been, thanks. For all that will be, yes.' Can you say thanks for the journey you have made in this beautiful place? Throughout this pilgrimage the inspiring figure and story has been that of St. Kevin. Whatever the actual facts are, the legends suggest a person who was prepared to say 'yes' to life and all it would bring. As you leave Glendalough are you able to say 'For all that will be, yes'?

The whole valley of Glendalough is like a cradle to which people constantly return as if it is their spiritual birthplace. Generations of families have their own stories of good times spent on summer Sundays here. *What will be your lasting memory?*

Our prayer for you is that you leave Glendalough feeling rested and revived, and that by exploring the valley and its story you have found affirmation of the uniqueness of your own spiritual identity. We hope you sensed all things in God here and have a renewed appreciation of the wonder of all creation. Most of all we encourage you to keep asking questions of life and stay with those questions, in the confidence that God has placed the answers you need deep in your heart.

Looking back for the last time toward the monastic city, the top of the round tower stands out pointing toward the sky. As we bring this story to a close it is autumn and the swallows are circling above the tower preparing for their journey to the southern hemisphere in search of the sun. They will return again in springtime to the exact place where they were born in order to start a new family. It is a reminder of how we are drawn back time and again, even in memory, to places and times and people that have been significant for us.

Why is Glendalough a place that people return to and where they find something new each time they visit? We all need special places to visit as a way of focusing on our special needs and intentions. There was an old pilgrimage tradition that seven visits to Glendalough were equivalent in spiritual grace and effect to one visit to Rome. Whatever the truth of that, an Old Irish poem expresses a wise insight about pilgrimage:

To go to Rome,
Is little profit, endless pain
The Master that you seek in Rome
You'll find at home, or seek in vain.

[Translated from the Irish by Frank O'Connor]

In a recent Irish language poem, Seán Ó'Ríordáin suggests *"Tá Tír na nÓg ar chúl an tí"* [the land of heart's desire is at the back of the house]. Perhaps the greatest challenge of all is to find what we are looking for in our own home.

Go raibh Críost agus Muire
Dár dtionlaic feadh an bhóthair;
Nára turas é in aistear,
Gura tairbheach gach orlach.

May Christ and Mary
Go with us to the length of the road;
May our journey not be in vain
But may every inch of it be for our good.

[Saltair: Fiannachta & Forristal]

Reading List

A.G. Leask, *Glendalough; Official Guide,* The Stationary Office, Office of Public Works, Dublin

John O'Hanlon, *Lives of the Irish Saints,* Vol 6, James Duffy & Sons, Dublin, 1891 [National Library, Dublin]

John O'Donovan, *Letters containing information relative to the Antiquities of Co. Wicklow, collected during the progress of the Ordinance Survey in 1838.* [Typed original copies in the National Library, Dublin]

Desmond Forristal, *The Man in the Middle,* Veritas, Dublin, 1988

Michael Rodgers & Marcus Losack, *Glendalough, A Celtic Pilgrimage,* The Columba Press, 1996

James P. Mackey, *An Introduction to Celtic Christianity,* T & T Clark, 1989

Esther de Waal, *A World Made Whole,* Fount, 1991

Nora Chadwick, *The Celts,* Penguin, 1991

Peter O'Dwyer, *Towards a History of Irish Spirituality,* The Columba Press, 1995

T.W.Moody & F.X.Martin [Ed.], *The Course of Irish History,* The Mercier Press, 1987

Pádraig Ó Fiannacha & Desmond Forristal, *Saltair,* The Columba Press, Dublin 1988

Rev. John Ryan S.J., Irish Monasticism: *Origins and Early Development,* The Talbot Press Ltd., 1931

Carmina Gadelica, Floris Books, Edinburgh, 1992

Edward Sellner, *A Common Dwelling: Soul Friendship in Early Celtic Monasticism,* Cistercian Studies Quarterly, Vol 29, No. 1, 1994

Thomas Berry, *The Great Work, Our Way into the Future,* Bell Tower, New York, 1999

Brian Swimme, *The Hidden Heart of the Cosmos. Humanity and the New Story,* Maryknoll, NY: Orbis Press, 1996

Richard Rohr, *Everything Belongs,* The Crossroad Publishing Co., New York, 1999